SO HOW DOES HE SEE THEN?

The story of Mac, a blind dog.

'the darkest nights produce the brightest stars'.

So How Does He See Then?

The story of Mac, a blind dog.

Debbie Jefferies

Acknowledgements

With grateful thanks to everyone who has helped Mac on his journey.

Mum, Damian, Sindy, Jo, Dee, Anna, Christina, Collette, Wendy, Lynn, and Nigel. Thanks for the moral support, financial support (from mum), the lifts, the help, the advice, the dog sitting. Thanks for caring, I know you love Mac as much as I do.

Also thanks of course to the staff at Bayview Vets, Dawlish. The nurses, receptionists and especially Rod McGregor BVSc CertVOphthal and CertSAS MRCVS.

Back cover 'Mac at the Groomers' photograph courtesy of Mary Gately, Bow Wows, Chelston, Torquay.

Prologue.

In August 2023, my beloved rescue dog Mac had his remaining eye removed. I immediately thought that's it, I've lost the Mac I knew. He's going to be a different dog. His life had changed in an instant. The thoughts that went through my head in those first couple of days were bleak.

He had been plunged into eternal darkness.

Never to see the sun again. He wouldn't even know if it was day or night.

Never to look into the garden and growl at the squirrels who dared to encroach on his territory.

Never to chase a ball or find his favourite toy.

Never to charge up the stairs, jump on the bed and sleep upstairs while he waited for the sound of the car, which meant I was home.

Never to watch the bees on the lavender and imagine eating them. (Mac was obsessed with bees).

Never to bark at or attempt to chase the neighbourhood cat, Dave.

Never to spot an item of food on the ground and pounce on it before I could stop him.

Never to 'see' his friends again.

Never to see my face, or jump on mum's lap, or jump on the bed.

Never to chase the squirrels at Oldway.

It sounds dramatic but this was how I felt in the first week after my sweet little rescue dog had his remaining eye removed. I was devastated. I felt as if I was in a nightmare. I remember that I was due to go to an old friend's birthday meal the day before Mac was going to be operated on, I was crying all the time, worried about how he was going to survive with no eyes. How I was going to cope. I gave myself a stern talking to.

Don't spoil Gill's birthday, it's her day.

The meal went well. I barely mentioned Mac, not wanting to bring my troubles to a celebration but I was the first to leave the restaurant. My friend Dee was looking after Mac, and I wanted to get back. I walked out without paying for my share of the meal. My mind only on getting back to my boy. (Don't worry, I settled up eventually).

I knew that Dee would have spent the evening cuddling Mac and crying. She adored him and she was one of his favourite people. He would have enjoyed his evening of being spoilt.

The uncertainty of whether he would adjust, would he sink into a depression, how would we manage? The thoughts just kept going round and round in my head, the situation we were facing felt overwhelming, as if he was going to be put to sleep rather than facing an operation.

Despite the first few pages, I don't intend this to be a depressing read. I wanted to chronicle our journey, the emotions I went through, my fears and worry concerning our future. I hate change and don't adapt easily to anything new or different. If you are facing the same situation please trust me when I say if I can do it, so can you.

I'm writing about Mac because I hope my experience will help other people who may wonder how they are going to cope with a blind dog. I've learnt a lot and if that helps just one person and their pet to adjust to their new way of life then I'll be happy. That is my intention and why I wanted to tell Mac's story.

I apologise in advance that as I have a male dog, in general I will be referring to all dogs as 'he' and 'him' rather than her, she, or them.

The unknown is frightening. You might think that you won't be able to manage. That your dog won't be able to come to terms with the loss of his eyesight. Please have hope. You will cope and so will your dog.

Don't give up before you've given yourself and your dog a chance to adjust. Trust me, you will. In six months' time you'll look back and wonder what you were worried about, your dog can still enjoy his life, his walks, his friends. He'll still play with toys. In a different way perhaps but he will still play.

Try not to dwell on the negative. Focus on what your dog can do, not what he can't do.

Sometimes I miss Mac's deep brown eyes and the way he used to look at me. Eyes are so expressive. It's not about the aesthetics, he is beautiful with or without eyes. It's when I see pictures on social media that people have posted of their pets and often the comment will be 'ah, look at those eyes.' Then it hurts a little bit.

They say the eyes are the windows to the soul and perhaps they are, but before I get too poetic, what about that song which talks about those lying eyes. Yeah. Tell it like it is, Eagles. (That's the band that sang 'Lyin' Eyes' in case you think I've lost the plot).

You can tell a person's nature by their behaviour. The sweetest souls shine through whatever they look like, whether you can see into their eyes or not. It's the same with animals.

I want to express how I felt at the time, my worries, emotions, and fears, even though I could laugh at them now. We have come such a long way in a short period of time.

Hope. A small word that means so much.

To give you hope, here is an approximate timescale of what to expect.

In only a week to ten days you will start to see a glimmer of light at the end of the tunnel. Walks become easier. Home life can be coped with. You'll think, I can do this.

In two weeks, you might be out on a walk and people will say 'isn't he doing well'. You will smile and reply, 'I know, and it's only been two weeks. You will start to realise that you will be able to deal with having a blind dog.

In six weeks' time, you and your dog will really be adjusting well to your new routine. Life is becoming much easier. When you meet people on a walk and mention that your dog hasn't got any eyes, they do a double take, bend down to take another look, unable to believe that your dog is blind.

Four or five months in, you may give yourself an admonishing rap on the knuckles, your dog is doing so well that you have both become over confident. You might not be concentrating on looking out for any obstacle, he is charging about regardless of walls, furniture, not waiting for you to give him the all clear.

Consequently he bumps into things, hurting his nose. He gets a fright, and you get a reminder that he still needs you to be his eyes from time to time.

In six months you and your family and friends will sometimes forget that your dog is blind. Life is almost back to normal, or the new normal that everyone in the family can cope with, having a blind dog has not impacted on your life as much as you had originally thought it would. You barely have to think about consciously watching your dog, it's automatic, it has become second nature to glance at him just to make sure he is not going to bump into anything, then to carry on with what you were doing.

Some experts say you should keep a blind dog on a lead for his own safety. I can say with the utmost confidence that if your dog used to enjoy being off the lead on some walks, he will be able to manage with just a little initial training. He will love it, it was part of his old routine, and he will enjoy his off lead walk as much as he ever did, so will you, watching your pet trotting around a park, sniffing, weeing, stopping now and then to process the information his nose is picking up, you wouldn't even know that he couldn't see.

You might be doing an off lead walk in a familiar place, as I was just this week. I went to a country park with my friend and her two dogs, we were chatting away, looking occasionally around to check that Mac was fine and to give him the odd verbal command. My friend said: 'look at him, doing his own thing. Mr Independent.'

Mac's tail was up, gently wagging, confidently enjoying his walk and all the sniffs around him. He always used to march off ahead of us and having no eyes certainly wasn't going to stop him changing his habits. He didn't act as if he couldn't see.

No-one would know, unless you told them, or they noticed his lead proclaiming 'blind dog' which was draped around my neck like a lanyard. He's got a collar which says 'blind dog' but no-one seems to notice that, especially when his coat has grown. Half the time his fur obscures the words. I haven't bothered to put it on him lately.

Have Hope. You'll get there.

If you want to go straight to the summary of the tips and advice, I have done a recap at the end of the book.

They See Everything.

I knew how much dogs observed the world and their owners. Dogs are watchers. They watch everything around them, monitoring, assessing, and judging. Is their den safe? Do they need to sound the alarm?

They look at you all the time, they watch your face, they recognise your expressions, they gaze at your eyes; what are you looking at? They notice micro expressions; dogs are experts at reading faces and moods.

They like to know where you are, what you are doing, where you are going and why you would even think about doing it without them. Nowhere is sacred. They have no respect for personal space. Why would you shut the door when you're going to the bathroom? If the door is ajar, you may be sitting on the toilet contemplating life, and spot an eye looking at you through the crack in the door, before they barge their way in. If you're lucky they will just stand there staring at you. If you are unlucky, they will rest their head in your pants which are currently residing somewhere around your knees.

Nice. Serves you right for not closing the toilet door.

Dogs are great observers, which is probably why they were domesticated by early humans. They can guard and protect territory, warn against enemies and predators, carry things, provide warmth, pull sleds. I thought that sight was the most important of their senses but actually it isn't. Their hearing is better than ours, ears twitching at the slightest sound, they can detect the faintest rumble of thunder in the distance well before we can, their acute sense of hearing, which is well beyond the range of human ears, makes firework displays a nightmare for some dogs and their owners, I've noticed that collies especially, have incredible hearing.

A dog's olfactory sense is greatly superior to ours. Some reports estimate that a dog's sense of smell is 100,000 times more powerful than humans. I can't even imagine that. It must be like another world within our own. Longer nosed breeds seem to have the best sense of smell. German Shepherds and Spaniels are often used to seek out whatever we need them to find. Bloodhounds, beagles, dachshunds, and retrievers also spring to mind. Apologies if I've left out your own breed of dog.

We use dogs to find drugs, explosives, currency, blood, contraband, missing persons; to detect bodies under rubble after an earthquake. We refer to them as detection dogs or sniffer dogs. It has been proved that dogs can be taught to detect cancer. Hunting dogs can be trained to differentiate between different prey or species of birds. Sight is possibly more important to hunting dogs and retrievers but even then, they rely as much if not more on their other senses.

Born deaf and blind, puppies find their way to their mothers' teats using a sixth sense like a heat seeking missile, guiding them to the teat where they can get warmth and nourishment. They are blind for the first ten days of their life and although they can see after that, their eyes don't develop fully for around fourteen weeks. They are using their noses, primarily, to scent their mother along with their super heat seeking ability. I believe that Mac has switched this sense back on. He can follow me no matter how quiet I'm trying to be, it's uncanny – or perhaps I stink!

From the smallest to the largest, once grown, most of the breeds are very alert, they see everything and stick their noses into everybody's business.

Outside, if a car door opened as we walked past, Mac would stop and look and wait to see if it was anyone he knew. Who is it? What do they want? Where are they going? Have they got a dog? He was so nosy it was almost embarrassing. Having no eyes hasn't changed his behaviour. When a car pulls up near us, he stops, faces the car, appears to be staring in their direction, obviously he is using his other senses and I end up urging him to move on, telling him it's nobody we know.

When I first got him he loved open doors; especially strangers houses, if he was off lead, he'd try to get into them to have a nose around. I wondered if it was because he had been a stray. Perhaps it's a survival technique. Getting to know your territory. Leave no stone unturned, explore everywhere, there may be food.

Once when we were in a dog friendly pub having a meal, I had put Mac's lead around my chair leg. Not securely, as it turned out. A member of staff emerged from the kitchens, holding Mac, asking, 'who did this black dog belong to?'

We were in disgrace. It was very embarrassing. I just hoped he hadn't tripped the chef up or managed to pinch anything. He was so fast. I could never catch him when he was off lead if he didn't want to be caught. He'd run round and round my legs taunting me. Incredibly fast, nippy little terrier, he would move slightly out of my grasp every time I reached for him. I'm sure I was a source of endless amusement for him and anyone else in the vicinity, watching a middle aged woman, red in the face, unable to catch her recalcitrant dog.

In The Beginning.

In May 2016 after three months of trying to find the right rescue dog — not too big, not too small, I was browsing on an internet site called Dogs Blog, which showed dogs in need of homes all over the country. I clicked on the picture of a little black dog. He was being fostered in Southampton and had been brought to the U.K from Romania by a charity called Paws2Rescue, who rescued strays at risk of being destroyed by the authorities. The charity saved as many dogs as they could afford to bring back; starving dogs, unwanted dogs, frozen dogs, dogs who had been cruelly treated and in danger of serious injury or death. As many of the unloved and uncared for as possible, were given a chance. They were neutered and vaccinated, de-flea'd, given pet passports and brought to the U.K.

In 1999 I had adopted a collie cross from Battersea Dog and Cats home in London and had fourteen wonderful years with her. I was devasted when she died in 2014 and thought I would never have another dog.

In my mind, no dog could replace Jess. She was so clever. She would bring us the post, put things in the bin, could play hide and seek. She invented games and showed me how she wanted to play them. On unfamiliar walks, having no sense of direction, I'd forget the way back to where I had parked, Jess would pull until I went in the direction she wanted me to go and would lead me back to the car. This happened when I was with a friend, neither of us could remember the way back and my friend said, she's just pulling to get back to the sea (Jess adored any water). Wrong. She led us straight back to the car. Once, on a new walk I was getting dangerously near to the cliff edge, blundering through trees and brambles, Jess pushed me over to the right path just in time. I hadn't realised I was feet away from a sheer drop.

Everyone loved Jess, she was such a character. Of course you can never replace a beloved pet and you shouldn't try but when you lose them, the emotion is so raw, you can't imagine feeling that amount of love for another animal.

If you've ever had pets, you'll know the sadness of losing an animal. They are one of the family. Their lifespan is just not long enough. I didn't want to go through that pain again, besides, I thought, no dog would live up to Jess. She was unique. She was special. She understood whole conversations, no dog would ever be as clever as Jess, she was almost human. I thought I'd end up comparing the new dog to Jess which wouldn't be fair.

In the days when dogs were allowed to sit anywhere in a car, she would sit in the front seat and once, when I accidently took a corner in third, She gave me a disdainful look, looked at the gearstick, then at me, before turning to resume her observation of the world outside the window. Her acute hearing had informed her that I had been in the wrong gear.

Yes, my dog had corrected my driving. Who needs a partner.

We'd have conversations. Another time we were driving to one of our favourite walks, Jess again in the front seat. I spotted someone walking a sweet golden retriever puppy, a cute little ball of fluff.

I said, 'aw, look at that puppy.' Jess looked out of the window and threw a growl over her shoulder, as if to say, 'puppies. Grrr.' She made me laugh.

Two years went past and while I never forgot Jess, I started to miss having a dog around the house. I missed our walks and our games. The fun we had. A walk in the countryside or on the beach was enhanced by the company of a four legged friend. Now, if I didn't have a reason to go out, I wouldn't walk every day. I was becoming unfit, plus I knew that stroking and cuddling an animal was good for your mental health. I would be physically and mentally healthier if I had another dog in my life and I knew that I could give an unwanted dog a really good home.

My mother and I shared our house, she was getting older and while she said she didn't mind if I got another dog, she felt she couldn't cope with an animal the size of Jess but would be happy to have a small dog.

I didn't realise how hard it would be to find what we wanted. I checked all our local rescue centres daily, logged into Battersea's website, I just couldn't find the right animal. We didn't want a tiny dog, or an energetic Jack Russell – the dog homes at that time seemed to be filled with Staffies, Jack Russell's, Chihuahuas, or bigger breeds. I just wanted a small mixed breed, preferably a dog which didn't moult as both mum and I had allergies.

Some of the Rescue Centres insisted on the whole family coming to meet the dog, every day for a week, to get used to each other. That was too difficult for us. Mum was in her nineties and not a good traveller, we couldn't even go as far as Plymouth without her getting car sick.

Three months passed and I went on holiday to Bournemouth for my sixtieth birthday. Getting changed in my pokey hotel room, I flung my black nightshirt on to the pillow, where it lay in a heap, then I took a photo of the room, which was the size of a walk-in wardrobe. I went to look out of the tiny bedroom window, the glass had blown, misting the window, making it impossible to see the sea, so much for requesting a room with a view. I thought.

Then I sent out a little prayer: Dear God, all I want is a little dog. Why can't I find a little dog? Please? It's not much to ask, is it? What about that line in the bible, ask and ye shall receive? Amen.

I thought, why am I standing here, feeling miserable, having a go at God.

Get a grip.

At least my friend Dee was travelling to Bournemouth, joining me for the last two days of my holiday. We had a great time, despite the accommodation and the weather.

Back home, I resumed my search, looking at Dogs Blog every day.

One afternoon in May, I clicked on the picture of a little black dog to find out more about him. From the image, he looked about the size of a spaniel. He'd been rescued from the death camps in Romania, his name was Poufy, and he was currently being fostered in Southampton. He looked cute, with such soulful dark eyes, I made a snap decision to apply to adopt him, certain that other people would get there first. I kept looking on Dogs Blog, not expecting to be able to adopt Poufy. After a few days, still searching on the internet, I picked another dog called Charlie. He was the one, definitely. I was very excited, until I found out he was in America. How did that get on my search? I decided to stop thinking about getting a dog for now. I was becoming obsessed.

A few days later, the phone rang. It was a stranger called Alison. She told me I was at the top of the list of people wanting to adopt Poufy and if I passed the house check, I could have him.

I could not believe it. I was so excited, but I didn't want to tell anyone in case it all fell through. A week went by, I passed my house check, then we had a last minute setback with our arrangements to collect him. My friend worked for British Rail and the two of us were going up on the train. The charity decided it wouldn't be safe as we didn't have a crate, we would either have to buy a crate or collect him by car. The only day that suited us both was that day, which was a Sunday. Nowhere that sold crates was open. My friend, who was determined I would have Poufy, offered to drive the four hundred mile round trip to pick him up.

I am so lucky with my friends. My father always said, you can count the number of true friends on one hand. I think I have a few more than that and I appreciate every one of them.

Anna had been the one to take me to Battersea to collect Jess, all those years before and here she was again, coming to my rescue.

We arrived at the foster house to be greeted by what appeared to be about fifty barking dogs, running around our legs, presumably saying hello, or go away, or stand still while we trip you up.

In reality, it may only have been about five dogs, memory plays tricks on you. Anna spotted Poufy immediately and fell in love, sitting on the sofa with him on her lap, turning to me and saying how gorgeous he was. I wasn't so sure. He was a lot smaller than I had realised, a small mixed breed terrier type with tiny legs and a very loud, deep bark.

'What do you think?' Anna whispered.

'Not sure.' I mumbled back. I wanted a bigger dog, at least the size of a small spaniel, not one with no legs – at least he didn't appear to have any.

Jess had been such a beautiful dog. I had fallen in love with her instantly. People would stop me and comment on how gorgeous she was, one man even offered her a lick of his ice-cream, really! One of our stranger encounters. She accepted, ice-cream being her absolute favourite.

Poufy was so different to Jess. I'd told myself not to compare him to her, yet here I was being shallow. It's not all about looks. Besides, every dog is gorgeous in their own way and in their owners eyes their dog is the most striking or cutest dog on the planet. The one with the best tail, the nicest colour, the cheekiest face, the ugliest, it doesn't matter, they all have something about them that we end up loving.

I couldn't back out now, not after all Anna had done for me. I supposed I would bond with him in time. I was an animal lover, it just wasn't love at first sight, like it had been with Jess. I'd spent months poring over pictures of dogs on the internet and being too choosy, Here was a little dog who needed a forever home and I knew I could give him a really good life.

We sorted out the paperwork, the foster lady said he had to wear a harness, not a collar and lead and kindly gave me one of hers.

This is the first key point. The charity recommended to all their re-homers to always use a harness. It was kinder for the dog. In hindsight, I wish I'd listened. It's always easy in retrospect.

I didn't realise that a collar and lead puts stress on the neck, especially if they pull, and this can affect the pressure in the eyes. I don't know if it can actually cause glaucoma but perhaps it can trigger it, in a dog who might be pre-disposed to eye problems. I will never use a collar and lead on any future dog again but, of course, I knew none of this or how our future was going to pan out.

Jess had never worn a harness, neither had Jason, my childhood spaniel. It hadn't done them any harm.

Once we were home I soon saw that Mac hated having his harness put on and would hide when he saw me pick it up, so I reverted back to collar and lead.

My first regret or mistake that would lead to Mac developing this horrible disease?

Anna and I emerged from the foster carers house and stood beside the car, looking at each other.

'He's so lovely, don't you think?'

Anna was besotted. I felt like saying, you have him then. Looking down at the little black dog currently peeing up my trouser leg. He wanted me and was marking me as his own. It appeared to be love at first sight for Poufy at least.

The fosterer had said he was almost perfect, and they had been considering keeping him and calling him Albert. I'd got him in the nick of time before they adopted him themselves. I was informed that the name Poufy meant small and fluffy in Romanian, I couldn't imagine calling for him if we were in the middle of a field in Torquay.

'Well I won't be calling him Poufy or Albert'. I told Anna. 'He's going to be called Mac.'

We drove back to Torquay. It was a hot day, and we stopped a few times for comfort breaks. The only thing that worried me was that Mac wouldn't drink. Looking back, I think it was a stress thing, he still doesn't drink when he is stressed. Jess used to get cystitis and I was worried about Mac not drinking.

We got home, my son had come round to meet the new arrival. He'd been completely besotted with Jess; they had adored each other, and I had a feeling that Damian didn't want to like Mac, but he couldn't help himself. The little dog lay on his back to have his tummy tickled, then went over to the corner of the front room and cocked his leg. Incidentally, that was the only time he ever pee'd in the house. He must have been marking his territory. Once on me and once in the house, to make sure he never lost his way.

Mac settled in as if he realised straight away that this was his forever home, he loved it and loved us.

That first night I put him in a basket next to my bed. I woke up in the middle of the night to find Mac lying on my bed making odd noises. Quiet yips and strange whines, it really sounded as if he was talking. It went on for some time. It might sound silly, but it felt quite spiritual as if he had a Guardian Angel and was telling her he would be all right now. I never heard those sounds from him after that night. His vocal range consisted of various barks, occasional howls, pants, and those sweet little dream barks dogs make, their paws twitching as if they are having the best dream ever.

Mac would try out all the beds and I often found him on my bed or on mums, both of us being a bit short sighted, we frequently mistook him for a black shawl lying across the pillows. I took a picture of him and remembered my holiday in Bournemouth.

Getting the snaps out, I couldn't believe it, at a quick glance my black nightshirt looked exactly like Mac when he was stretched across the bed. It appeared that God had a sense of humour, he had sent me an image of Mac and I had unknowingly taken a picture of what my future dog would look like, after saying my petulant prayer.

Honestly. That photo is uncanny.

My nightshirt on the bed in a hotel, one month before I got Mac.

Here to Stay.

Mac was the complete opposite of Jess except where language was concerned. He seemed to pick up English so quickly and understood so much. He's such a clever dog, I couldn't have imagined that a mixed breed terrier would rival a collie for brains, but he did. I hadn't had a terrier before and quickly discovered that they are very stubborn. He'd stop walking if we weren't going in the direction he wanted and he often decided when it was time to return home by pulling me back the way we had come. Actually Jess used to do that too, perhaps they realised that I was a bit of a pushover. I would give in sometimes and let them have the walk that they wanted.

Mac had firm ideas about who should take him out (mainly me) and would refuse to move if I wasn't going to go as well. The chosen few were allowed to take him out which seemed strange to me as he loved most people, but he is definitely a 'mummies' boy'.

When I first had him he would check the weather before a walk and decide if he felt like going out. He wasn't listened to of course, as we never missed going on one of our three main walks a day. It's not just about the exercise, it's also about them needing to do their business. Having a routine, your dog quickly gets used to having a poo in the morning and another on the afternoon walk. Mac likes to squeeze out an extra poo in the afternoon, we call him Mac Two Poo. Every dog is different of course! My son says I'm obsessed with Mac's bowel movements, needing to know if he has been and wanting to have a description of the consistency.

I don't think I'm that strange. A lot of my friends are the same with their dogs. We need to know if their diet is right for them and not upsetting their tummy. We all love a good firm poo. A perfect Linda McCartney sausage (other brands are available).

A lot of dogs don't like defecating on their home territory. I only have decking as a back garden and Mac won't even wee out there, I wouldn't mind but he does.

I think it's important to have a routine and good for your dog to have all his senses stimulated with a variety of different walks around the area.

Love, exercise, routine and food, the key to a happy pet. I should add discipline, the key to a happy owner!

At home Mac would hide his treats and bones all over the house. Bones seemed to stress him out. He couldn't eat even a small one, but he didn't want anyone else to have it.

He wanted them but they were hard work. His jaw and teeth perhaps not strong enough to tackle things like bones or antlers. They'd be placed under mattresses, down the sides of chairs. In fact there is still one somewhere in the house that we never found. Who knows where that went. We don't buy bones any more, small treats please him more, something he can eat immediately.

Mac soon charmed everyone he met, and we all fell in love with him, once I'd come to terms with the fact that he didn't look like Lassie. He was cute and had a magnificent fluffy tail that strangers would remark on, and no-one could resist his deep soulful eyes.

Taking him to my local veterinary surgery for his first check-up, the vet thought he was around two and told me he had arrythmia, which I hadn't known. I looked it up and it did say that he may grow out of it. It hasn't been mentioned since, so either it causes him no problems, or he has, indeed grown out of it.

When you take your dog out, people often say hello to your pet.

'What is he though?' I would get asked by complete strangers.

'Some kind of poodle.' They'd say before I could speak. 'Schnauzer.' Strangers speculated.

'He's a shiatzu, definitely.'

Dee thought he looked like a cocker poo crossed with the dragon from an old film called The Never ending Story.

I had his DNA analysed and waited excitedly for the result. When it came I could bore strangers with the facts over and over again, reciting the various breeds that made up my dog.

'Poodle, Cocker Spaniel, Schnauzer, Black lab ...'

'Black lab? No way, my friends said. He doesn't play with balls, and he doesn't retrieve.

'Bearded collie and several unknowns.' I added.

I could understand the Bearded collie. Mac liked to herd me. Jess had been a border collie crossed with a rough collie; she'd liked to herd me too.

Strangely, the DNA results showed that all the breeds they had found in Mac, were pre-disposed to eye problems.

In appearance, I thought he was mainly cocker poo with a pinch of miniature schnauzer and a dash of shiatsu.

At first, although he adored most people especially our family and close friends, he was timid and would try to run away if he was doing something I didn't agree with.

For example, once off lead he dashed over to beg for food from a picnicking couple. Before I could ask them not to give him anything he'd managed to acquire what looked like two meatballs, secreted them one in each cheek before charging off to stand twenty yards away, watching me, and pretending he had nothing in his mouth. I'd chase him, trying to get them out of his mouth (well, they might contain onion which is poisonous to dogs). I could never catch him. He used to do that a lot. Find food, then stash it in his cheeks. Hamster had not been present in his DNA results.

Any time I had suspicions that he'd been scavenging, which was quite often in the summer, we live in a tourist resort and people don't always clear up after themselves. I'm being polite here. Ilsham Green was often strewn with disposable barbecues, cans, sweet and crisp packets, half-eaten burgers, or other unidentifiable food. Most of the visitors arrive in cars, I don't understand why they can't clear up after themselves, put the rubbish in their car and find a bin or take it back to where they are staying. Locals go out and litter pick, but we shouldn't have to.

In our favourite country parks, people having picnics on the grass, seemed to just throw the food they didn't want, tossing it a few yards away, perhaps thinking they were leaving it for the birds. I'd notice Mac, snuffling away in the long grass, suddenly stand to attention and look at me. It was a dead giveaway. That guilty look.

We'd stare at each other, me trying to work out if he had food in his mouth, Mac pretending that nothing was further from his mind. There was no way he was concealing half a sausage roll in his mouth.

Nothing to see here. He seemed to be trying to convey to me mentally. Move along now.

The longer we continued the stare off the more certain I was, that he was hiding something, eventually putting my hands in his mouth (to his disgust) to remove whatever it turned out to be. He used to warn me off, in the early days. Thinking about it, I suppose it's the height of rudeness, inserting your fingers into someone's mouth to remove a delicacy.

Funny that. I'd forgotten he used to growl at me. I would call his bluff, correctly as it turned out, he would never follow through and snap or bite.

Once, in a beer garden I'd let Mac off the lead to have a little potter about, he headed straight for the flower borders and emerged with a large, battered onion ring in his mouth. He looked like a bull with a ring through its nose, this thing hanging out of his mouth. It was a great prize and I spent ten minutes chasing him around the garden before I managed to get it off him.

If he scented a bitch in season, he'd be after her even though he'd been neutered, he didn't know he was firing blanks and took up the pursuit eagerly. He was quite frisky, any young dog was fair game, male, or female, as long as they smelled nice he was quite happy to hump them.

He spent a happy hour with a dog called Basil one summer evening, chasing each other round and round the cricket pitch, both of them trying to hump each other. It was a one-time only fling, they never met again.

Mac would go up to anyone sitting on a bench. He'd jump up, snuggle between them as they would coo and say how cute he was. He knew it and he played on it.

He was scrounging of course, during the tourist season, most people sitting on benches had some food and he wasn't fussy. Sandwich, pasty, pork pie. No matter how much he ate, he seemed to stay around the eight kilo mark probably because he was such a live wire.

One of Dee's first memories relating to Mac was of me telling her that he was from Romania, and he hated the rain. If he heard it, he'd pretend to be asleep so, he thought, I wouldn't make him go out.

Dee thought to herself, oh no, he's moved to Devon, where it rains six days out of seven - or so the saying goes. Mac hated his coat too and if he saw me pick it up, he would run and hide. He's never liked getting wet but has always loved being wrapped in a warm towel, cuddled, and dried.

In the beginning, he didn't understand toys and wasn't interested. He was nervous of household objects, and if you got the hoover out, or a broom or any stick-like object he would run away, we presumed he'd been hit in his old life.

Mum had an aid that helped her to pick up things. We called it the grabby. If she picked it up, Mac would disappear.

His first toy was a little yellow chick, eventually he grew to love it. It went everywhere with him and became more bedraggled and dirty by the day and was often added to the weekly wash. He soon had growling tug of war games with chick, octopus, and various other toys, occasionally retrieving them, bringing them back for you to throw again.

He wasn't bothered about balls. I think he had poor eyesight even then in a 'tracking a ball' kind of way. However he always spotted a cat or a squirrel before any other member of his pack, he could see well enough for that, not to mention discarded food, dropped or thrown on to the grass.

One of his first canine friends was a female miniature labradoodle called Chilli, they would play wrestle and chase, flying around the field, Mac jumping over grassy hillocks as if he was a champion hurdler. Passersby would watch him and laugh; it was a sight to behold. I think he would have been good at agility even though he was so small. He was fast and he could hurdle. Chilli and Mac adored each other until Harley joined Chilli's family.

Harley was a young blond energetic cocker poo, full of himself. He ruled. Only he was allowed to play with Chilli. Mac was pushed out. It was a difficult few months. I felt like Mac had lost his best friend. I don't think Chilli was too bothered.

If we went to our friends house, Harley and Mac would fight over toys, bones, food, anything left on the floor. Blankets, beds would be fought over. Any basket Mac lay in, Harley wanted and vice versa.

Outside, Mac liked to dig. They'd get into a fight over the hole – both wanting to dig in the same place. If Harley thought Mac wanted a stick, Harley would fight him for it.

To be fair, as I now know, no other dog in Torbay, possibly the world, is allowed to carry a stick, only Harley. If he isn't stopped, he will attempt to take one from any passing dog. He is pack leader and possibly King of the canines.

Mac was never really bothered about sticks, except in the bad old days, when he and Harley would fight over anything, simply because the other one wanted it.

If we were invited to Sindy and Jo's house, we'd have to watch the dogs all the time to try to stop fights before they happened. If we forgot, distracted perhaps by an exciting game of cards, suddenly a fight would break out under the table, because Mac had put his nose too close to Harley's favourite toy. It was distressing for us and the dogs.

One time, on a walk, a long stick got caught in Mac's harness, before Mac had time to panic, Harley charged past and extracted it. No stick was allowed to be carried by any other dog whatever the circumstances.

 After a year or so, Mac and Harley became best mates. Harley adored him and would kiss him over and over. If they met unexpectedly in the park, they would run towards each other, whining with excitement, and entwining themselves around each other's necks. It was charming to watch. Harley still gets very excited when he sees Mac and kisses him for at least five minutes. He also gives me a hello kiss, the minute he gets in the car. If on a rare occasion I turn up without Mac, Harley barks in my face letting me know his feelings on the matter. Telling me off for not bringing his pal.

They'd team up on squirrel hunts, (no squirrel was ever harmed or cornered or caught) chasing and running back to each other as if checking in. Mac was Harley's wingman. Chilli played as well but was more content to walk with her owner.

Chilli could be moody and grumpy. None of our dogs enjoyed being pampered at the dog parlour even though Mary the groomer was brilliant and always told us that our dogs had been so good. Chilli would take it out on us when she came out. How dare we have her washed, her fur cut and brushed. She hated going to the groomers and when we picked her up, she sat on the back seat of the car next to Mac. He sniffed her and got snapped at for his trouble. He was very upset and snuggled closer to Harley for comfort.

Going to the groomers always put Chilli in a bad mood. She didn't want to smell of perfumed shampoo, she wanted to roll in some fox poo or an old cow pat and would, at the next chance she got. So there, Chilli probably thought, I'll make you regret spending that money, you should have gone to the pet shop instead.

Mac grew in confidence and stopped flinching when mum or I picked up a broom or got the hoover out. He just took himself out of the way. He was laid back and content. He loved the routine of his life, two small walks and one main afternoon walk every day, rain, or shine. Breakfast and dinner at regular times. Mac was also a big fan of sleeping and once, when we took him with us on an excursion to Dartmoor too soon after breakfast, he sat on the back seat of the car, sulking and refusing to have anything to do with anybody for a good hour.

We live in a three storey house. Mum sleeps upstairs, we share the lounge and I sleep downstairs. Mac sleeps wherever he wants, on beds, in the armchair or in one of his two baskets. He knows he is adored.

He soon worked out my work shifts and would be waiting by the door when I was due home. If we told him we were going shopping, his expressive fluffy tail would droop, and he'd take himself off and curl up in his basket until we returned. Then it would be …. Coffee time!

Mac got a special treat at coffee time. It got to a point where you couldn't say the 'c' word in his hearing because he would expect something nice to eat. A dried fish cube or one of the special treats from the good pet shop. The good pet shop incidentally, where he went shoplifting with his canine friends not long after he lost his sight, more to say about that later.

If coffee was late, he would jump up at mum expecting her to say to me, 'are you making a coffee?' He was the same at dinner time, ganging up with her to nag me to get the dinner on.

His intelligence started to shine through, without training he decided of his own accord to become somewhat of an assistance dog. My mother was quite deaf and if I called her, she rarely heard me. Mac would charge up the stairs to find her and bark or jump up to tell her she was wanted. If she slept in, the moment I called, he would run up the stairs and jump on her bed to wake her up. He seemed to be saying 'Debbie says it's time to get up'! My word is law apparently and he considers himself my number two.

He is like a bossy manager at work. Keeping an eye on us and making sure we don't miss anything. If mum called me in the night, he would be the first to fly up two flights of stairs, barking loudly. We were needed. He would stand guard until I got there, somewhat slower.

He monitored the garden. Why weren't we outside seeing off the squirrel or the cat? If he could open the door, he'd do it himself.

If someone is at the door he has a special bark. If the phone rings, he has a different bark, which increases in pitch and volume the longer the phone remains unanswered. Mum calls the phone bark 'yapping and yowling'.

Jess used to make a similar noise when the phone rang, she quickly associated it with adventures, usually it would be one of my friends ringing to ask if I wanted to go for a walk, which they often did on a warm summer evening. She would push me to the phone and almost seemed to be saying, answer it quickly, it might be for me. She tried to take the receiver off the cradle once. She'd decided she would answer the phone as I hadn't been quick enough. I presume she understood that she would be able to hear what the person on the other end had to say, then she would act accordingly. Although she hadn't worked out how to convey to the caller that a dog had answered the phone. As long as she recognised their voice she could go and get her lead, before barking at me expectantly.

I still have a landline as well as a mobile phone, sorry to all you youngsters who have no idea what a landline is. Trust me, some don't. I've been told that my landline number can't be right, it doesn't have enough numbers!

Mac was really good with people and children. He didn't chase joggers, or bikes but he was quite reactive on the lead. He'd bark if he saw a dog walking towards him and would try to fling himself at that dog. I couldn't seem to stop him doing it. I'd cross the road, but he'd fling himself around like a feral firework. He didn't like big dogs on or off lead and would run at them and bark. I had to be very alert if he was on an off lead walk as he would end up being the dog that would come off worse.

Once, he'd been pinned down on the beach by a large Rhodesian Ridgeback who'd taken offence at being chased and barked at. Mac squeaked but didn't learn his lesson. The next day, if he saw a dog he didn't like the look of, he'd do it again.

Another time, in Cockington we were walking up from the lakes, and we heard a bit of a dog fight going on, rounding the corner we saw about five big dogs at the top of the path, going for each other. Mac, naturally, decided he was going to join the fight. He didn't know any of them, but he wanted to be in the thick of it. He started to run towards them, and Harley blocked him with his body. Mac tried to run round Harley and Harley blocked him again. The pack leader, deciding it would be too dangerous, telling him to stay out of it.

I think Mac thinks he's the size of a Rottweiler. When he cocks his leg to scent mark, he tries to get as high as possible, edging up steep grassy hillocks until he can get his scent as near to the top as possible. Beware all you other dogs, I am the biggest dog in the world, and this is my territory – I presume he is thinking.

There May Be Trouble Ahead.

One evening, we were returning home after our last walk and Mac spotted Dave, the cat who lived a couple of doors away. He flung himself towards the cat, taking me by surprise, he's very strong for an eight kilo dog. He spun round and hit his head on the bumper of my car, which was parked in the car port.

I probably wasn't very sympathetic and said something like, 'I bet that hurt, that was silly, for Heaven's sake Mac, if you didn't pull like a lunatic, you wouldn't have hurt yourself.'

A few days later, my friend and I noticed that his right eye looked a bit cloudy. I took him to the vet, and they gave me some drops.

Two days later, his eye started to turn silver and bulbous. We went back to the vet and was referred to an animal clinic quite a distance away. I can't remember much about that time. I know it was in the winter because I remember the consultant at the clinic saying that I could call them any time, even Christmas day because Mac had glaucoma. It was serious and if his eye got worse he would be in a lot of pain.

The vet said, imagine the worst migraine you've ever had. That's what he will be feeling. He had to go to this surgery once a month, stay in overnight and have his eye pressure checked every hour. He hated it and always had an upset stomach the following day.

I blamed myself. I'm sure that Mac bumping his head on my car had triggered the glaucoma. If only I'd seen the cat and taken more care, making sure that Mac couldn't hurt himself. But he was so fast, flinging his body around before I even knew what had happened. I know it wasn't really my fault, glaucoma is often genetic, but I still felt guilty.

The vet was very nice to us both, she hoped we could keep both eyes healthy for as long as possible but refused to give me a time frame. It couldn't be predicted.

Glaucoma was more difficult to treat in animals than it was in humans. I was told. It only ever had one outcome.

I should say that If you are reading this and your dog has got glaucoma but hasn't lost their sight yet, remember that this is our personal journey, each dog is different, and it may be possible for your dog to have laser surgery or shunts fitted to prolong their sight. Each case is unique, unfortunately this wasn't an option for us.

I was told that Mac might be fine for a year or two or even longer but usually the outcome was bleak. He would lose his eyes. She impressed on me the importance of doing his drops every eight hours no matter what and to come in regularly to have his overnight eye pressure tests.

At first I couldn't do the drops. Mac wouldn't stay still, and I spilt more that I got in his eye. Friends helped until I got the hang of it. The best schedule for me was 5 a.m., 1 pm and 9 pm. I was an early bird, rather than a night owl. I set the alarm for five in the morning and as soon as Mac heard it, he would jump on the bed to have his eye done.

For the lunchtime one, he would leap up onto mum's lap, as good as gold and let me do his eye, while she held him. Then he got a piece of cheese for being a good boy.

I liked to have at least three bottles of the drops. One to keep downstairs, one to keep in the lounge and one in my bag in case we went out for the evening. I was determined that I would not forget to do his drops at the right time.

I did my best for Mac and apart from doing the drops three times a day, I mostly forgot about his eyes. He was loving his life, enjoying walks with his friends, still hating walks in the rain but spotting a squirrel made it all worthwhile.

I put the knowledge that Mac had primary glaucoma to the back of my mind. If I did think about it I was optimistic. I had the medicine, I didn't mind doing the drops for the rest of his life, he was going to be one of the lucky ones. I felt sure he was going to keep his sight.

One day I noticed that he wasn't his usual happy self. My friends always examined his bad eye, telling me if they thought it looked cloudy. I thought they were imagining it.

I wanted to think they were imagining it. It was the light that's all. In daylight his eye looked ok. I remember that I was always saying to Sindy, do you think that Mac's eye looks cloudy? I'd lift him up and she would look at him intently before telling me what she thought.

He was fine. His eyes were fine. Perhaps very slightly cloudy but the drops were working their magic. No need to worry.

There was a need to worry. He wasn't himself. He was in pain. One morning his right eye went silver and bulbous again. Emergency trip to the vets. It was horrendous, to know he was in pain, questioning if I should have brought him in sooner. This time there was no way back from this, he was booked in to have his right eye removed.

Back home, I was in a bit of a state. I posted on the charity website, many people responding, telling me he would be fine. Dogs coped really well with just one eye. I thought it was going to be awful. I think people thought I was over-reacting, not my family or friends of course, they all loved Mac and worried alongside me.

Please, if anyone reading this is going through the same thing, dogs *do* cope with just one eye. I was over-reacting. Don't worry, your dog will be fine. He doesn't know that he has had an eye removed. His brain quickly adjusts to having one eye. He will appear to see as much as he ever did.

In our case, I expect Mac had been in some pain for a long time and might have had limited vision anyway. Once he'd got over the operation, it only took him about five days to regain the spring in his step. He carried on as before. There was no noticeable difference in his behaviour. He often spotted a squirrel to chase before his two eyed friends.

I hadn't needed to put myself through such stress. Mum and I had spent the day of his operation sitting in the front room, crying.

Now I had to focus on keeping his remaining eye healthy.

Drugs, Drips, and a Drop of Hope.

The medication came in small bottles, expensive and didn't last long, especially if Mac moved at the crucial moment and I missed his eye. Ordering more was sometimes like trying to get hold of a marketable drug. They wanted me to bring Mac in for an appointment and request another bottle in the flesh, rather than ordering more over the phone. Did they think I had another dog with glaucoma and was trying to avoid paying two consultation fees?

The receptionist would question why I wanted two bottles and said she didn't think the vet would allow that. I wondered what they thought I wanted to do with them? Flog them on the street corner? Was there a street value for eye drops for dogs? They were expensive to start with, what did they think I would sell them on for? Did drug dealers or addicts deal in canine eye drops? It seemed very strange to me. I spent more time pondering this question than was strictly necessary.

I started to think that they just wanted me to take him in for the more expensive twenty four hour pressure check, then they could charge me accordingly. I have no idea whether this was standard procedure or whether in fact it could delay the progress of this horrible eye disease. At the time I thought that I could tell by Mac's behaviour how he was feeling, whether he was in pain or not and by looking at his eye to make sure it didn't seem cloudy. I suppose I thought that I knew my dog better than the vet did and that I was doing what was best for Mac.

In retrospect I think I should have erred on the side of caution. I wish now that I had done everything that they had asked of me and not missed a single overnight pressure check appointment. Everything is easier in retrospect. It's natural for human beings to go down the 'if only' route.

I can't change things now … wait for it, an over-used saying, 'it is what it is'.

Much later, I was told by the last consultant we were seeing that I should examine Mac's eye by shining a torch into it, telling me what it should look like, however I knew none of this then.

I felt that sticking rigidly to my drops routine was keeping the disease at bay.

My lovely female vet had moved on to pastures new and I didn't feel so comfortable with the new consultant I was seeing. I delayed the next overnight appointment. The drops were doing what they should. Mac seemed fine; I didn't see why I should pay a lot of money for the twenty four hour pressure testing. I didn't like being separated from him and he hated it. I thought that keeping him stress free was better for his health. I also didn't have good insurance and was on the minimum wage, it was all taking a toll. I just wanted to take Mac in for a normal consultation, get his eye checked then bring him home. They wanted him to stay over-night every four to six weeks. Eventually the vet refused to prescribe the drops without having Mac in. My choices were becoming limited.

The clinic appeared to relent and offered to test him if I brought him in early in the morning then I could take him straight home. Brilliant, I didn't have to leave him.

That suited me, apart from the drive through rush hour traffic. The older I get, the less confidence I have, driving. I don't know why. Maybe it's just an age thing.

The hour long white knuckle drive done, the vet thoroughly examined his eye, told me his eye pressure was fine. Now they wanted me to make the appointment to have him monitored for 24 hours, oh and would I bring his food in – a new development, another cost cutting venture on their part. Well done. I applaud whoever came up with that idea, oops sorry, sarcasm slipped in there.

I felt conned. The whole point was to avoid that. I'd now been charged the consultation fee and health check fee only to be told I had to come in again for the more expensive 24 hour monitoring, the next week.

His eye was fine. Why did I have to go back again so soon? I felt that I was trapped between a rock and a hard place. I'd only found two places my local vets could refer me to, the place I was currently attending or one in Bristol and there was no way I could drive to Bristol.

I want to repeat that this was how I perceived things to be, this is how I felt at the time. I certainly won't name this particular clinic, most of the staff were so caring and wanted to do everything they could for us. We were also in the latter stages of the pandemic, a very difficult time for all of us.

It's hard for pet owners. Vets are becoming more and more expensive, so is pet insurance especially as your pet becomes older. We would all like to have the best possible treatment for our loved ones. I was becoming paranoid and suspicious, thinking that it was all about the money. Most folk don't like change when it's going to affect their pocket.

There are two sides to every story. People who work in the veterinary field, work hard, the majority are kind, caring, sympathetic and do their absolute best for your animals. I don't know what it costs to run an animal practice, all I remember is how I felt at the time. Perhaps the reasons weren't being explained to me. The animals being treated and having to stay in at the surgery might not have been eating. A lot of food may have been wasted, perhaps it's better for the animals to stay on the diet they are used to.

Regarding asking for more medicine, no-one told me why I couldn't have two or three bottles of drops when I tried to re-order. Perhaps they only had a limited stock.

No-one explained why Mac needed a more thorough appointment so soon after the last one, when they had informed me that his eye was fine and there had been no change.

Some members of the public need a longer explanation, if they can see a valid reason for it, they wouldn't feel as if it was all about money. I wish now that I had just taken him in every time they had wanted me to, but I don't know if it would have made any difference in the long run.

I'd looked up primary glaucoma on the internet, tried to research it but I probably didn't understand exactly what was happening or what would happen. I added certain foods to Mac's diet; carrots and mushrooms in small amounts were said to be beneficial. When we had the initial diagnosis, my lovely vet explained the importance of always using a harness, she told me why.

I stopped using a collar and lead once I'd had the explanation of why a harness was better.

So here we were again. I was picking him up after his stay. The consultant was busy, but a friendly nurse explained that his eye pressure was good. She told me that there was nothing to worry about at the moment however the consultant wanted him to have a new additional drug. These had to be kept in the fridge.

In my head that translated as, there is no change. Mac's eye is stable, the pressure is normal, but we want to make you pay for more medicine.

Nothing was explained. Why did the consultant want him to have a different drug on top of the ones he was already having? He might have been doing everything he could to keep Mac's eye stable for as long as possible. Perhaps new research had shown it might delay the progress of glaucoma. That didn't occur to me at the time, and no-one ever explained.

This new drop had to be given at least ten minutes after the last evening drop. I asked the nurse if she had done the 5 a.m. drop. Looking at her notes she told me it had been done around six. I argued that when Mac had been prescribed these drugs I had been told how important it was to stick to the eight hour routine. I was really annoyed. My original vet had impressed on me the importance of doing the drops every eight hours. The nurse assured me that it didn't matter.

I have no idea whether it did or not. I think there was a lack of communication all round. My advice is, for anyone going through something like this, make a note of all the questions you want to ask and think carefully about what you need to know. Keep asking, new research may have shown that it didn't matter as much as originally thought. Things change. Perhaps they knew that with primary glaucoma there was only one outcome and that his time was running out but maybe they didn't want to leave me without any hope.

Revolving Doors: sub-title: Me going on a bit about our routine.

I wasn't going to mess up Mac's schedule. I decided to do the new drop, which I called the fridge drop, about ten minutes after the 9pm one. Everything now revolved around his medication. If we were going to friends for the evening, I had to take the two lots of drops, put one in my friends fridge, make sure I set the alarm on my phone, it was a hassle, but we managed. The fridge drops were in an even smaller bottle than his normal drops, they weren't going to last five minutes so I got on the phone to order a spare and went through the usual 'I don't know if the vet will allow you to have one. We will ring you back – usually one or two days later. Then, because I hated the drive, I would ask for them to be posted. Incidentally, I wonder how drops that have to be kept in the fridge can travel through the postal system in a normal envelope?

Answers on a postcard please.

I'm joking. It's probably fine until they have been opened.

I won't say much more about that period except that eventually the fridge drops became drops that didn't have to be kept cold, but I still called them the fridge drops, even though I didn't keep them in the fridge any more. Following me so far?

If someone was minding Mac for me (mum couldn't do the drops) I'd have to give them written instructions with the times and what treat he had afterwards.

I remember Dee saying, 'so after his lunch time drop he has a piece of cheese? What does he have after his fridge drop?'

The fridge drops we now kept in a yellow bag, but the name had stuck.

'Give him anything, it doesn't matter.'

'I want to give him what you usually give him. I'm writing it down and pinning it on my board.' My friend, the perfectionist said.

We carried on in this fashion for about two and a half years. I'd been lulled into a false sense of security. I still believed that Mac might even go through his entire life and not develop full on glaucoma. Although I think his eyesight must have been getting worse. He fell down the stairs from top to bottom several times. At the time I put it down to him, taking the stairs at his usual speed and missing his footing.

Game Over.

One Friday morning I called Mac, ready to go out for his first walk and noticed he was behaving strangely. He was disoriented and appeared totally blind. He was in a state. Not knowing which way to turn and started to go round in circles.

I rang the clinic in a panic, asking if I could bring him in.

The voice on the other end of the phone said, 'who are you?'

I told her.

'I can't find you on our system. You'll have to go to your own vet; we only take referrals.'

'What?'

I'd been getting all of Mac's medication from them for two and a half years. They'd operated on him. He'd had many of the over-night stays. The nurses, when I returned to pick him up always used to tell me how sweet he was. I remembered my lovely Australian vet telling me that if I had any concerns to ring them day or night even if it was midnight, even if it was Christmas day there was always someone there, and I would be able to bring him straight in.

I could not believe it. Now they didn't know who I was. They'd never heard of me, or Mac and I wasn't able to book him in for an emergency appointment.

I managed to get in to my local surgery that morning and they discussed options, Bristol was mentioned then they remembered that there was now an eye specialist in Dawlish, and they would refer us. I don't know why the original clinic was not mentioned but I didn't care, I was desperate to get Mac seen and I was lucky that Dawlish had a cancellation, and the consultant could see me that afternoon.

My friend Sindy came with me for moral support and to help me find the surgery, another drive I hated. Once in Dawlish itself, the streets are narrow and quite steep. We eventually found the surgery and I met the consultant.

Mac had recovered from his totally blind incident and appeared to be back to his normal self. Obviously his eye wasn't good, but I hoped it was just a blip and we could carry on as normal. Rod McGregor the consultant examined him and dropped balls of cotton wool on the floor.

'He saw that'. I said, watching Mac intently.

He definitely saw that.' I repeated, more for myself than the consultant.

Rod tested his eye pressure. It wasn't good. He suggested I increase the drops I called the' fridge drops', to three times a day.

Oh Lord, our life was going to be nothing but drops and it was going to be expensive, the way I did it. I think I complained a bit, whined that I missed getting the drops in his eye half the time and wasted some of the precious fluid.

Rod was the first person who showed me the best way to hold Mac and how to do the eye drop in such a way that spilling any was almost impossible. It was so easy. Why hadn't I worked out how to do it like that myself?

The vet told me to come back on the Monday. I tried to make the appointment when I left but I was told they had nothing free and to ring later in the week to try to get a cancellation.

We had a good weekend but on the Monday Mac kept shaking his head, he was obviously in pain and seemed to be trying to clear his eyesight. I rang Dawlish but it was an extremely busy surgery, they'd had no available appointments or cancellations, and they couldn't fit me in until the end of the week, when I finally got to see Rod. Mac had had another incident where he had gone totally blind for ten minutes and panicked.

We did the cotton ball thing again.

'He definitely saw that.' I said, clutching at straws.

Rod hmmed and said mildly, that he had asked me to bring him in at the beginning of the week. I said in my defence, that I'd tried and was told they had no vacant slots.

Rod took out his eyeball and gave me a lesson. By this I mean, he produced a large plastic model of a dogs eye, unscrewed it, and showed me exactly what was wrong with Mac. He said he would try an infusion. I was to leave Mac; the procedure would hopefully bring the eye pressure down. It was dangerously high, in the eighties, when it should be around ten.

I got the impression that the eye specialist we were seeing was a very clever man. He seemed at home teaching; I didn't know if he did teach but he certainly had a knack for it. He was patient and explained what was happening every time Mac's eye pressure rose. This was the first time I was actually told, in detail, what was happening in Mac's eye. At the time I took none of it in, of course, being either in tears or on the brink of tears. I'd been so certain that Mac would be the one dog with glaucoma who would live out his life without succumbing to total blindness.

We left Mac and went for a walk around Dawlish with Sindy's two dogs while we tried to decide whether to wait or to come back.

'What did he say?'

'I can't remember. He got his eyeball out ...'

'What?'

I tried to explain but I hadn't really taken anything in. Sindy peppered me with questions, why hadn't I asked this and why hadn't I asked that? What options did I have? I know I had asked the consultant, but I couldn't remember exactly what he said. She said she would come in with me next time. I was obviously not to be trusted.

We decided to go home and wait for a phone call then go back to collect Mac later. I felt cautiously optimistic. Mac had never had an infusion before. I felt sure it would have a positive result.

Leaving the surgery car park, it was one way. The way out was up a narrow steep road and coming out at the top was horrible, I couldn't see if a car was coming, I just had to pull out and hope for the best. How the people who lived or worked in Dawlish did it every day I had no idea. It was horrendous. I say again, I'm not a confident driver.

A nurse from the practice rang me later to apologise for not fitting us in sooner. Rod had explained to the staff that Mac was an urgent case, and he must be seen, no matter what.

I once again had an ally in the veterinary world. I felt that we mattered.

The following week we were back again. The extra drops were helping. Rod had told me exactly what to look for.

I had to examine Mac every day, shine a torch in his eye and look at the pupil. I would be able to tell if the drops were doing their job.

Why had nobody told me this before?

Then began the many trips to Dawlish. I rang all my friends begging them to take me.

'I can't drive to Dawlish. I can't remember how to get to the vets.' I would lie.

Christina took me once. She had to bring her two big dogs, planning to walk them after I'd dropped Mac off at the vets. It was bucketing down, we got soaked. After the walk, we managed to find a café who didn't mind two dripping wet humans and two bedraggled dogs and sat there drinking coffee and tea while we rang the vets to see when Mac would be ready. Not until late afternoon it transpired.

Christina couldn't bring me back later; she had an appointment. I begged a lift from my friend Jo.

When we got there Jo said that Sindy had told her she had to come in with me and gave me the list of questions I was to ask. I was obviously not to be trusted to attend the appointment on my own, quite rightly I think.

'He might get his eyeball out.' I told her, hopefully.

Jo looked at me, askance.

The consultant didn't disappoint. He showed us what was happening with Mac's eye, using the plastic teaching aid. Mac had primary glaucoma, he also had strange optic nerves. His was a very complicated case. Every time the eye pressure rose, it caused more damage. I imagined it like a lightning strike. Damaging another part of his optic nerve. Rod said that they would try another infusion on the Friday. It had worked the last time and was worth giving it another shot. Rod had dropped cotton wool balls in front of Mac again and I was sure that Mac had followed the movement and still had some sight left.

At home, Mac fell down the stairs again. He could go up them but not down. I blocked the stairs so that he couldn't attempt to go down on his own. I carried him when it was bedtime. Mac slept downstairs with me. He has to be where I am, he's a real mummy's boy.

This time the benefits of the treatment lasted a day. I was told to take Mac in to discuss the options. I was about to live my nightmare.

No-one was free to drive me to Dawlish on the Friday. I had to grit my teeth and do it myself. My friend Sindy was the only person free to come with me and she came in to the consulting room to make sure I asked the questions, and she was there to remember the answers. An operation to put a shunt in might not work. It wasn't just about providing the necessary drainage; Mac's optic nerve was either too damaged or a more complicated problem than I realised. Deep down I knew that I shouldn't put Mac through a difficult and possibly painful operation, which may not work, certainly not long term. I was clutching at straws and not being realistic.

I was in tears most of the time, I think. Poor Rod, he gamely carried on, trying to ignore the fact that I was in bits. I just couldn't bear the thought of Mac going blind. I thought we were going to be one of the lucky ones. No matter how many times I'd been told that glaucoma was a horrible disease in dogs and that blindness was inevitable, I thought we'd get away with it, even if he could just make out shapes or see whether it was day or night we would manage. I had been blithely optimistic, so certain Mac was going to live out his whole life with one eye and enough vision to keep his funny, bossy personality.

I think Rod said we could try the infusion again. I can't really remember.

Everyone knew that Mac was going to have to have his remaining eye removed.

Rod suggested leaving Mac there and he would perform the surgery that same day. I wanted to have the weekend to come to terms with it. To enjoy Mac for a little longer while he could still see. To have one more walk in one of his favourite places, which he loved, even with the limited vision that he now had.

I stood at the reception desk waiting as the staff tried to find a slot the following week and a surgeon who could perform the operation. It was Rod's last day for three weeks; he was going on holiday.

I know I was standing at the desk, unable to stop crying.

Sindy next to me, was telling me that it was inevitable, why was I delaying it? She thought it was silly to put it off, best to get it over and done with. Mac was in pain.

Rod popped out of his consulting room; he must have heard us debating. He repeated his offer to operate on Mac that day then I could take him home in the evening. Take Mac home that is, not Rod.

I really wanted it to be Rod who performed the operation. I had faith in him, obviously a very clever man, a top eye specialist and surgeon.

Every time we had been in, all the nurses and staff had taken great care of Mac. I liked this surgery, not the position of it, admittedly, argh, coming out of that road, I still have nightmares.

Mind you, driving in to Dawlish main town there is a very good bakers where we usually just had time to stop and purchase something for breakfast or brunch.

Every cloud and all that.

I left Mac at the surgery to have his operation.

My friend Dee came with me to collect him. They'd thought he would be ready to be taken home at three but when we got there they said he needed more time in recovery, and it would be nearer to six.

Not wanting to do the drive again, Dee and I wandered aimlessly around Dawlish, looking but not really looking, in the shops. Eventually we went and had fish and chips in a café near the harbour before walking slowly back up to the surgery.

Dee sat in the back of the car with Mac. I think we both cried all the way home. Dee loved Mac to bits, and he looked so sorry for himself. The eye socket stitched and bandaged.

I have a vague memory of Rod hearing me say that Mac was in perpetual darkness now.

He assured me that blind dogs could adjust. He would start to use his other senses more. Sight wasn't as important to dogs as it was to humans. Their sense of smell was incredible and so was their hearing.

I was thinking how I would feel if I suddenly lost my sight.

Rod said that vision wasn't the most important sense in a dogs world. How I was imagining it would be for Mac wasn't how it actually was.

I heard what he was saying but didn't really take it in at the time.

My family, friends and I cried for the dog Mac had been, the live wire who ran everywhere and jumped up to sit next to you, the dog who was as fast as lightning, running across the fields, his ears flapping, mouth open in a canine grin, looking like a little cartoon dog. The dog who chased squirrels and cats if he could get to them. The dog who gazed at me all the time as if I was the most beautiful person in the world. Unconditional love.

I mourned the loss of his eye. It was almost like a bereavement, and I needed time to grieve for the dog that he had been.

That may sound dramatic, but my world revolved around my little dog. Mum was in her nineties, and I was her full time carer, she was very good for her age but after a couple of bad falls was quite frail. It had been a difficult few months.

Two close friends had died earlier that year, one unexpectedly and one from cancer. I had spent as much time with her as I could. We had been friends for over forty years. I missed them both so much.

My son had a bad accident on his motorcycle and took months to recover, breaking at least five bones in his body and tearing a tendon. He was out of work and that was a worry too.

Enjoying my walks with my friends and Mac was my release. I've always loved animals especially dogs and enjoy being out in the countryside or on the beach. Having a dog beside you, enhances the walk for me, watching them having fun, enjoying all the sights and sounds or should I say, sniffs and sounds, seeing the world through their eyes (I can't stop referring to vision) adds to my pleasure.

Game Over. New Balls Please.

That first week I found it very hard to imagine how I was going to manage. I had to watch Mac constantly, so that he didn't walk into things or fall down (or up) steps or kerbs. Walking slowly around the village I met a lady who told me that her dog hadn't adjusted to being blind and she'd had her put to sleep. One of my friends had said that I might have to consider that myself if I found that we couldn't cope. But how long had that lady given her dog before she came to that awful decision?

Another person I met told me the same thing. Her dog hadn't been able to find his food bowl, she had felt it was too difficult for both of them.

In retrospect perhaps they could have tried other things. I don't know. Every dog is different, and I didn't know either of the people well enough to ask.

Mac was the same at first, he couldn't find his food bowl. You'd think his nose would have led him straight to his dish especially as he was quite a food orientated dog but no. He didn't like putting his mouth into a deep bowl even though he'd always done it.

Perhaps it felt different when he couldn't see what he was doing. He would bump his nose on the rim of his bowl then lose confidence and refuse to eat. I hand fed him at first, then put his food on a flat plate.

He wouldn't drink from his water bowl but would drink from a bottle outside, again I experimented, cooking chicken, and giving him some of the juice in a shallow dish. Try different things until you find what works. Mac will now drink out of his water bowl but has his dinner on a plate, because I had immediately given his food bowl away instead of waiting a couple of weeks. No need to be hasty, give it time.

He will also drink and eat from one of those plastic takeaway containers. I discovered this by accident when a friend gave him some chicken and juice in one she had kept. He finished it quickly then picked it up. We laughed and gave him a biscuit. When I told him he was clever, he must have thought, oh good, I'll do it again then, I'll get a gravy bone. Now of course, it's his nightly trick, performed on command, to get a biscuit. Then repeated as often as he can in the hope of another treat.

The first few days were extremely difficult. Mac couldn't find his way around the house, he would constantly bump into the table or a chair, lose his confidence and stand still, not wanting to move at all. This is a house he has lived in for the last seven years, I really thought he would know his way around it blindfold, as they say. I didn't think he'd have a problem in the home that he knew so well. It turned out that the house took longer for him to get used to than being outside.

This is where a scent trail would help. Mac could always find his way back to his basket, his refuge and safe place.

We put bubble wrap around everything, so that he wouldn't hurt himself when he bumped into things. We were able to remove it after only a week. It's important to make things as safe as possible for your dog and try not to move the furniture around so that he remembers where everything is. At first he might be extremely slow and wary, not wanting to move. It's tempting to help him by putting him on a lead or picking him up. It's quicker for both of you. This is not a good idea. He will become independent sooner if you don't mollycoddle him.

The same with food, I hand fed Mac for a couple of days then encouraged him to eat from his plate, otherwise I would still be doing it, Mac liked nothing better than being given tempting morsels of moist chicken or freshly cooked fish. He adores being fed by hand. Spoilt little boy.

Walks took forever. Mac kept stopping and refusing to move. He had no confidence at all. If anything brushed against him, even a weed sticking out from the wall, it frightened him, and he would freeze. The walk that used to take us twenty minutes now took at least forty. My eyes were glued to the pavement, watching out for loose paving slabs, or looking ahead, anticipating where the next obstacle to negotiate, was.

That first week I seemed to meet everyone who'd ever had a blind dog or knew of a blind dog.

'Oh, you'll be fine', an acquaintance told me, 'we had a blind dog. It was no big deal.'

He was so blasé about it, as if he wondered why I was even slightly bothered, it comforted me.

'He'll soon adjust.' A stranger told me, 'there's a blind German shepherd that we see in Cockington, she still chases a ball. She finds it by scent.'

I am talking about a dog by the way, not a person from Germany who is looking after the sheep residing in Cockington. On another tangent, last time we went to this country park, some sheep had got out of the fields and were roaming all over Cockington – no shepherd or farmer in sight!

A relative said, 'Auntie Ruby had a blind dog. She used to shout, 'stop bumping into the furniture'! Not very nice! But it had been a long time ago. Perhaps people were more matter of fact about these things in the old days. Or unsympathetic.

I bought a white lead that had the words Blind Dog on it, to warn strangers that he might bump into them. Don't bother getting one of those halo things, that fit around the head or neck, yes they warn the dog if he's going to bump into something … by bumping into something with the halo. What's the point? In the narrow streets of Devon we would cause havoc with one of those. Besides, when I tentatively asked Rod if he thought it might be a good idea he just shook his head and laughed. I guess that's a no then.

Week one: I told a stranger we met on our walk about Mac's operation. Her reply: 'So how does he see then?'

You would not believe the amount of people who said the same thing.

Really.

I wanted to be sarcastic, my natural response in most situations, but she was a nice lady, so I just smiled.

It reminded me of an advert around at the time. Man has anti dandruff shampoo in his bag. People say, 'I didn't know you had dandruff?'

He said, 'I don't'.

'How does your dog see then?'

'He doesn't.'

Doh!

Bohemian Rhapsody.

I'd decided it would take Mac a month to six weeks to get used to being blind. If I was having a bad day, I'd think 'he'll be so much better by September.'

At first, I began driving Mac to Ilsham Green where he could have his early morning walk off lead, in was quicker for one thing. The walk around the village was torture and took so long.

Ilsham Green was a wide expanse of grass with nothing for him to bump into. Although he would stand in the middle of the field disorientated now and then, but as soon as I called him, sang, or clapped my hands he'd run towards me. I was still getting up early, my body clock conditioned to waking up at 5 am. We would head out as soon as it was light, both of us ready for the early morning walk. To help Mac know where I was, I talked all the time. When I couldn't think what to say, I sang, loudly and not very tunefully, Queen songs mainly. They have a huge back catalogue of songs and I'd been a big Queen fan in the seventies and eighties.

Bellowing out, ironically, 'don't stop me now, I'm having such a good time …' while hoping that nobody in any of the nearby houses could hear me. If they did, they probably covered their heads with a pillow, thinking 'oh no, that nutter's in the field again, and wishing that they could 'stop her'.

At some time during the first ten days, my friends Jo and Sindy took Mac out to give me a break. They went to Walls Hill, another off lead walk, they told me that they walked backwards the whole way round, watching Mac and trying to encourage him to keep walking. They said they sang a made up song containing the word Macadoodle, (clearly they weren't Queen fans) for the duration of the walk, so that he would know where they were, until they were both sick of the sound of their own voices. It's funny now, we've come such a long way. At the time I couldn't envision doing a normal walk again.

Back to the first week and Ilsham Green, strangely, I kept bumping (not literally) into another couple who had been at the Dawlish surgery. I'd noticed them in the waiting room with their spaniel, on the same day as I'd taken Mac in for his operation. I think their spaniel had injured one eye on a branch in the wood and it had formed an ulcer. They had to keep the eye dry so they couldn't do their favourite beach walks. The water loving spaniel would have been straight in the sea.

We saw them again when we went to one of the cafés in Dawlish for a coffee. Now I was seeing them most mornings, even though it was early – before seven. What a small world.

In the evening, Mac's last walk of the night was around the block. In August the council did not cut the verges, consequently some weeds were nearly three feet high, sticking out, the slightest brush of a weed against him, would startle Mac, who would then stop and refuse to move. On the second day after Mac's operation I had taken my secateurs and cut back as many of the weeds as I could, to hopefully stop them from brushing against him, making him jump. There were too many though and it didn't make a lot of difference, eventually he would only jump slightly then move on.

He kept veering towards the walls on the other side of the pavement opposite the verge, then banging his nose. I was trying to keep him in the middle of the path until my son told me that was where Mac wanted to wee. He wanted to pee up lamp posts or trees, against the walls or fence posts, where he had always cocked his leg before. Plus, the edges were where the best sniffs were. Most male dogs liked to pee against something. I had to guide him slowly to the wall so he could reach it safely, without banging his nose. He was instantly happier. I was doing what he wanted.

When you are being their eyes, you notice how many hazards there are, bins put out on recycling day, lamp posts, trees, brambles, unkempt verges, branches sticking out, big stones, pot holes. It has given me such an insight into what blind people have to deal with every day. How do they manage? Massive admiration to them and to guide dogs.

When Mac had even limited vision he paid no attention to any signal I might try to give him with the lead. He also didn't seem to use his nose much.

Jess used to play 'find the biscuit'. She would wait in the kitchen with her back facing away from me, like a child covering their eyes to play hide and seek. When I had hidden the biscuits I would call 'find the biscuit' and she would run excitedly into the lounge and sniff them out.

Mac didn't play that game. I knew that he could use his nose, he could smell cheese the minute I got any out of the fridge, or if I dropped a tiny smidgen on the floor but he appeared to rely on his vision and his hearing primarily.

Back to our walk. I noticed that I was holding the lead with one hand and with the other, was holding it half way down, nearer to his head, instinctively pulling the lead towards me slightly when we came to something Mac needed to avoid.

I realised that Mac moved towards me with even a slight pull in the direction away from a hazard. Which he'd never done when he could see. He was adapting. Paying attention to everything I was doing, however slight.

Combine this with talking to your dog, however silly you might feel, talk to him all the time. Now that he can't see, he will be listening. I promise you; it will pay dividends.

A short lead gives you more control and your dog can feel where you want him to go. I haven't tried an extendable lead, but I don't think they would work. Your dog wouldn't be able to feel the signals and you might not react quickly enough to pull him away from danger. Having said that, I have seen a person using an extendable lead walking their blind dog and it didn't seem to cause them any problems. Experiment to find what you and your dog are most comfortable with.

If you have two dogs, your sighted dog may well start guiding and giving your blind dog confidence. You might even consider adopting another dog especially if your own dog seems depressed and used to love playing with his own kind. You would need to take it slowly; the re-homing centres would help and advise I'm sure. Pick a calm, gentle, confident dog, take time over the introduction, perhaps take them out for a walk together to see how they inter-act. Some centres may allow a trial period, maybe foster to start with to make sure both dogs are happy. Just an idea. I have seen this work.

Harnesses, collars, or coats stating 'Blind Dog' warn others that your dog cannot see them or their dog, if they have one. Then hopefully they will move out of his way if he is off lead.

Unfortunately they don't always notice and occasionally walk straight into Mac expecting him to move out of their path. Not everybody pays attention to their surroundings.

I have been guilty of that in the past. I'm also not the most observant of people and once threw a ball back to a blind man, expecting him to catch it without me saying a word. He was out with his guide dog, giving the dog some time off in a nearby field to run and play. I hadn't noticed the man's white stick. I still cringe with embarrassment at the memory when the ball hit him unexpectedly in the chest.

If you are doing street walks with your blind dog, this is how I started teaching Mac, We had gone back to walking round the village due to the fact that we'd had a lot of rain, and the fields were boggy, muddy, and not nice for either of us.

Once we were out of our street we had to go across a road.

I would tell Mac, 'we're crossing the road.'

If you have to step off the pavement, say 'down', repeatedly. Tugging slightly downward on the lead.

When you reach the other kerb say 'up.' Keep saying it, until he does it, pulling upward on the lead. Once he is on the pavement, praise him.

'Clever boy. Good job, Mac. You're such a clever boy.'

He responded. He liked being praised. His tail was up, and his confidence grew. He *was* a clever boy. He appeared to know when we were across the road, sometimes stepping onto the pavement before I'd had a chance to say 'up'. I have no idea how he knew but somehow he sensed it or knew how wide the road was.

Our normal routine prior to Mac losing his sight usually involved an afternoon walk with my friend Sindy and her two dogs, Harley the lively cocker poo, Mac's best mate, and Chilli the miniature labradoodle. I thought that they might want to do their own thing, as we were quite slow, but Sindy said it would be fine, she could always do walks that had a more difficult terrain on the days that she didn't meet us.

Some of our regular walks were not practical for Mac, I thought, in those early days (he does almost all of them now). We needed to go somewhere open, as flat as possible so that Mac could be off the lead with his friends. I wanted to give him the freedom that he'd always had. As much as was safely possible.

We tried two walks to see if he could cope. One was to one of the woodland walks that we liked. Brunel woods was a good place to go when everywhere else was muddy, it gave you some shelter and had a mainly gravel path. However it was a hilly walk, with hazards right, left and centre, literally. It was impractical. Mac had to stay on his lead, the route was not very wide, plants, nettles, and brambles on the one side, a sharp drop on the left. On the narrow path, branches were sometimes in the way or stones had been dislodged and lay there ready to trip up the unwary. It was difficult and I had to watch him every second, concentrating on steering him away from any hazard, moving branches or stones to one side before he got to them, instead of relaxing and strolling through the trees as we used to do before Mac lost his sight.

We'd nicknamed Brunel the haunted wood. Actually I could write a chapter about events in this particular place even when they could be explained. The latest escapade involved Harley who would always try to get into any field or fenced off area to see what was in there. He was the nosiest dog I'd ever met. He'd managed to get through a hole under a six foot fence, without us seeing. We called and called, thinking he was chasing squirrels before we heard frantic barking and crying coming from the other side of the very high wire fence which had a notice saying, 'Keep Out'. I'd jokingly said, that's where Harley will be then, not for one moment thinking he had found a way to get in there.

He had then proceeded to fall into a pit and couldn't get out. His cries becoming more distressed by the minute. We were panicking and couldn't see how we were going to get in there to help him but thank God other people walking their dogs appeared and Harley was rescued by a kind dog walker, who scaled the fence, got him out of the pit unharmed and sent him back to us. Actually, the man said he had jumped into the pit which had frightened Harley into doing an extraordinary leap out of the pit and finding his own way back with a little encouragement from the man. This had been a route we hadn't done before and one we definitely won't do again.

Previously, on more than one occasion, unexplained things had happened to us in Brunel woods as we passed a certain place; a dead duckling on the path (where had it come from? We weren't near water), a large branch falling with a loud thump to our left despite there being no wind. The weirdest occurrence being a headless pigeon which fell from the sky narrowly missing hitting us as we were walking along. I jumped and Sindy leapt about a foot off the ground. Perhaps we should apply to go on Most Haunted.

Oldway, which used to be one of our favourite walks, was also impractical. Lots of trees, posts to walk into, steps to negotiate.

At Oldway there was a copse of trees filled with squirrels. Most of the dogs headed straight for that area. It was the best fun ever. Looking for squirrels to chase. It used to be one of Mac's favourite walks.

The squirrels could afford the exercise, lots of people liked to feed them and there were always nuts on a tree stump or around the bases of the trees. They were so used to be chased I sometimes felt that they tested the dogs, running up a tree then immediately coming down the other side to appear behind them.

Those first two weeks I thought I would never do either of those walks again. Our first attempt at doing Oldway had been difficult. It had taken ages for Mac to climb all the steps and when we got to the squirrel wood, he wanted to charge off with his friends. If he had been off lead, he would have run straight into a tree. It wasn't much fun for either of us.

I drove to our afternoon walks. Putting Mac into the car, he would squirm and panic. Once I dropped him and he missed the seat. Then another time, getting out, he unexpectedly leapt into my arms when I wasn't ready and banged his head. Getting in and out of the car was becoming difficult until my son reminded me to tell Mac what I was doing.

Talk to your dog. This is so important and will help them to adapt quickly.

In the past, Jess and Mac had watched me constantly. They understood what I was doing, could anticipate what I was going to do next. If I looked in their direction, unless they were asleep they were always watching me. It might sound so obvious but of course it makes sense. Dogs with vision will watch your every move. They see that you are about to get ready for a walk, see you unlock the car. They know that this is a walk you are going to drive to. They are anticipating what is going to happen next. Usually excited. Yay, we're going out.

They know they are going to get in the car. Watching you opening the door or lifting the hatchback, they know that they are going to be put in the car or that they will jump in.

Mac needed to be told everything step by step. He can feel you putting his harness on but what are you doing next? I tell him everything.

'We're going to see Harley and Chilli. I'm putting my coat on. I've just got to get some poo bags. Let's get your lead on. Time to go.

I'm unlocking the car. I'm going to pick you up now and put you in the car'.

It instantly made a difference. I couldn't believe it. He was calmer and he understood what we were doing, where we were going and who we were going with.

Mac had a good sense of time. He knew when he should be going for a walk. He knew when I should be preparing dinner. If I was late with the evening meal, he used to stand in the kitchen doorway observing. He wouldn't move until he was sure I was cooking, and that the evening meal was underway. He acted like a Victorian husband, who expected his dinner ready and on the table at precisely six p.m.

If things weren't proceeding as fast as Mac desired, he would go over to my mother and jump up at her, as if he wanted her to nag me or at the very least, assure him that dinner wouldn't be much longer. It was hilarious.

We underestimate dogs. They are so much brighter than we give them credit for. How many times have we heard people say, 'if only they could talk'.

Thinking about food, it reminded me of an incident with Jess, who always had a spoonful of yogurt on her breakfast. One morning mum had prepared her breakfast. Jess wouldn't touch it, instead she went over to where mum was sitting and stared at her without blinking. Jess usually bolted her food; mum didn't know what was wrong. Was she ill?

No. Her breakfast wasn't up to its usual standard. Mum had forgotten the yogurt.

Mac couldn't see if I was going into the kitchen to begin cooking, so I had to remember to talk to him all the time. To tell him what I was doing or about to do. This sounds a bit daft, but Mac liked to know what I was doing, so why not tell him? Besides, he's the only one in my household who can hear me! I would say things like:

I'm going to start dinner. Dinner won't be long.

We're going for a walk now.

I'm going to put your harness on.

Won't be a minute, I've just got to get my shoes on. Wait.

Tell him what you are going to do all the time, even if you feel silly doing it. Your dog used to watch you, he anticipated your next move, If you picked up his lead, he knew he was going on a walk without you saying anything.

He doesn't have that now. He can't see what you are doing. Talk to him about everything.

Going out in the car: If you have a bigger dog that you can't lift, guide him gently into jumping into the car, hold your hand above his head so that he doesn't bump his head on the car.

With smaller dogs that you can pick up:

I start by saying exactly what we are going to do.

'I'm going to pick you up. Now I'm going to put you in the car.'

It worked. Mac knew exactly what was happening. He positioned himself slightly, ready to be picked up and because I told him I was putting him in the car, pressing his side against the back seat so he could feel where he was and didn't panic and fall off, he was fine.

We went to collect our friends. Mac curled up on the back seat until he heard them coming. Harley barking with excitement as they headed towards the car. Harley would get in, kissing and sniffing Mac as he'd always done. Giving extra attention to his bandaged eye socket, sniffing it to determine what had occurred. Chilli followed suit, then sniffed his willy, and licked it just once, as was her fashion.

Mac seemed to have a very attractive scent to most dogs and sometimes they wouldn't leave his bits alone. He didn't like it at all and would bark loudly trying to get them to go away, but he allowed Chilli the privilege.

Those first couple of weeks we tried most of our walks to see how Mac would cope. Walls Hill, which Mac knew well should have been ideal, but it had a lot of quite deep holes, large areas filled with very long grass and prickly shrubs. I had to watch him all the time, keeping him off lead except when we had to negotiate more tricky areas.

Harley would run all over the place, never still, exploring everything, looking for sticks or discarded food, chasing the birds or finding a like-minded dog to play chase. Chilli preferred to walk close to Sindy, taking her time and stopping frequently, which meant that Mac would walk straight into her.

'Chilli's bum.' Was the phrase most commonly heard on those walks as Sindy informed Mac what he'd bumped into.

Chilli is a beautiful girl, but she is not very tolerant. Growling, snarling, snapping, or barking if any dog invades her space.

She is amazing with regards to Mac. She has never turned on him once since he lost his sight. She has never told him off for walking into her.

How can she know he can't see? She must do. So does Harley. He doesn't rush over to gather his wingman to join in with his mischief. I find that sad, that they can't play like they used to but I'm getting over it. There is no point thinking about what Mac can't do. It bothers me more than him. Harley still loves Mac. He is always so excited to see him and the greeting they give each other is so sweet.

In unfamiliar places your dog will still bump into things. Let them do it under your control. You don't want them to hurt themselves, but they are creating a mental map of their surroundings and soon adjust.

The lead walks were getting easier, even after just two weeks. I would use key words. 'Careful'. 'Up', 'down.'

I would tell him if we were near a tree. 'Careful. There's a big tree.' You might think it's a bit stupid. Did your dog know the name for a tree before he went blind?

Mac is very clever regarding language. He picks up on my conversation really quickly. I think he understands.

Ten days after his operation we had to go to our local vet to have the stitches out. That was horrible. The vet struggled to remove them. Two of us had to hold Mac still and he really cried. It must have hurt. Once that was done though, he was fine. The operation site looked a bit red and sore but soon calmed down, his hair started to grow over the area, and you couldn't tell at a glance that he didn't have any eyes. Sometimes he appeared to be looking at me.

Off lead, he'd march off in front, tail up when we were on familiar territory, but he would be listening for me constantly and I watched to make sure he wasn't going to walk into anything. More key phrases that he understood. Along with 'Careful'.

 He now responded to 'this way' and 'over here' and 'no, Mac, this way, find Harley (or whoever we were with).

If I could see someone approaching with a lively dog, I would say, 'there's a dog coming, he's going to say hello.'

Mac would stop ready to be sniffed and to sniff back.

I would put him on his lead to go up or down steps, even then, be very careful. Hold the lead firmly. The first time, Mac went down one step then decided to take a flying leap down the rest. Luckily, there were only three.

Mac was still unsure at home. There were a lot of obstacles. Tables, chairs, the fireplace, the television on its stand, the sideboard. An elderly person in her recliner chair, her footstool, her bag of knitting next to her. Mac would bump into them all the time. It didn't hurt him but shook him up a bit. He would stand still waiting for me to guide him around to wherever he wanted to go. In the early days I was probably over-protective, not realising that he was mapping his surroundings which might have been why he took longer than I expected to get used to where everything was in our house. He was still shaking his head quite a bit. I wondered if he was trying to clear his eyesight, after all, he doesn't know what has happened only that he can't see. Maybe that will pass in time.

He sleeps more now and is often in a deeper sleep than before. Perhaps because for him, it is dark all the time, or perhaps because there are no visual distractions. He isn't able to look out of the window.

Of course, he is getting older, I think he will be ten this year. Maybe he would be sleeping more anyway.

When I tell people that Mac has had both eyes removed, the next thing they ask after 'how does he see then? Is to ask how old he is. I wonder if they think it doesn't matter so much for an older dog. I don't think of Mac as a senior. He doesn't look it and he certainly doesn't act it, apart from liking his sleep. He's a fast walker and I'm always trying to walk at his pace on lead walks. We are not crawling along at a snails pace as we did in the first week after his operation. I remember thinking at the time, that walks were going to take forever, and they wouldn't be a pleasure for either of us. How wrong I was.

I read something on the internet that said blind dogs take about six months to come to terms with the loss of their sight.

Three months after Mac's operation. We went to Brunel woods again. Difficult terrain, obviously trees to bump into, narrow paths, steep slopes on one side. Mac did the whole walk off lead. Responding to verbal commands, 'stay on the path', 'this way', and a sharp 'no' or 'careful' if he was in any danger. I said that if there was a dog version of the cub scouts, he'd just earned his 'off lead advanced walk' badge. He was amazing.

We tried Scadson woods, another walk with a lot of hazards, mainly a steep slope going down to a stream on the left hand side of the path. Mac coped admirably, again by listening to my instructions. For some reason, he wanted to walk on the edge of the drop to the stream, instead of staying on my right, the safer option. Obviously, the best sniffs were on the left and he was determined to go where he wanted to go. For safety, I put him on the lead for the most dangerous parts.

Two months later, he did it all off lead, moving to the safer side as soon as I told him. On the narrow part of the trail the most danger came from Harley, who was determined to carry a stick the size of a small tree and bashed into all of us as he charged up the path. Mac realised from Harley's growls that he was armed and dangerous and he and Chilli stayed well back until the thug had gone past.

Now when I told him there was a tree, he understood the word. I was repeating 'careful, there's a tree.' I could see that if I didn't stop him he was going to walk straight into it. He slowed, then walked gingerly up to it. I'd told him it was there, but he still wanted to sniff the base of the trunk and register his presence with a cock of the leg.

We were on Preston beach the other day. It's a nice flat beach with hard sand, Mac's favourite beach. He ran, jumped up at me, which he always does when he is excited. Chasing me, asking for a biscuit. I ran away from Mac so that I could kick Chilli's ball for her without accidently kicking Mac. I was fast but he was on my heels. If I changed direction so did he. Sindy was calling out 'he's behind you.' Like it was panto season.

I gave up, bending down to make a fuss of him as he jumped up at me, tail wagging. Good game, good game.

A lady with a boisterous young dog was coming towards us, I told Mac there was a dog about to jump on him, explaining to the woman that Mac had no eyes.

'So how does he see then?' She asked.

With difficulty, I would imagine. I thought.

Perhaps she thought I was exaggerating; he didn't act as though he couldn't see. He didn't look like a blind dog.

To be fair, looking at Mac, you couldn't even tell that he didn't have any eyes.

Another friend said that a passerby would never know he was blind. He was confident, sniffing everywhere and enjoying his life. He appeared to be looking around, his eyebrows twitched, at a glance you wouldn't notice that he had a disability.

We visited a friend the other night. She gave Mac some biscuits, then stretched her hand down to stroke him. He moved out of the way. He didn't want to be petted; he wanted another biscuit. She tried again, before her hand could touch his head, he moved back again. How did he know she was about to stroke him? We still don't know. Did he sense a slight change in the air with the movement of her arm? It's quite uncanny.

On Walls Hill Chilli wanted me to kick her ball. Again every time I tried to run away from Mac to play with Chilli, he followed me, getting in the way, jumping up. He was like a homing missile. How did he know where I was? Whichever way I went, he changed direction and found me. I wasn't clicking or rattling or singing. Maybe he could smell me.

He always wanted to be with me. If I asked him to wait with Sindy while I went to the poo bin, he would change direction and follow me, no matter how quietly I tried to walk.

Our morning routine has changed slightly simply because Mac doesn't sleep on my bed any more. He doesn't have the confidence to jump up. He tried once or twice in the early days and fell. Occasionally I lift him up so we can have a cuddle, but I don't leave him on the bed all night in case he wants to get down while I'm asleep.

I know that some blind dogs jump up on beds and sofas with ease. It just depends on the dog. I expect there is a way to help them learn how to do it but as Mac seems quite happy to be in his basket I'm not going to attempt it just now.

He knows the second I get up, even when I'm trying to be really quiet. He gets out of his basket, stretches, tail wagging then proceeds to make my life as difficult as possible.

I sit on the bed to get dressed. I try to put my socks on, he winds himself around my legs, jumping up, getting in the way. Getting my underwear on is apparently even more exciting. He must stop me at all costs. Trousers? No chance. It takes me ages to get dressed. Sometimes I collect my clothes and tiptoe to another part of the room and attempt to get dressed there. That doesn't work, Mac just changes direction, finds me, and jumps up. It's a good job I'm not usually in a hurry. I'd love to video myself getting dressed one day, it must be the funniest thing ever. Might be too revealing though, which is why I haven't attempted it yet.

Mac has always been a happy little dog and that hasn't changed. He loves his food and his friends, dislikes the rain but will tolerate it. He still barks at dogs he doesn't like the smell of.

A boxer dog walked past us in Cockington last week. Mac took exception to his scent. All four feet left the ground as he bounced and barked, seeing him off. Warning him to move away. Tail high, he looked like that cartoon skunk off the telly. Unfortunately the boxer had long gone. Mac was facing the hedge, barking at nothing. It was so funny. Another video moment missed.

One snippet I did film. The three dogs accompanied us to their favourite pet shop. I wanted to buy a coat for Mac, and I needed him there to try it on.

It was dog Heaven. All the smells.

Behind our backs, Harley, who had made thieving his career and was at the top of his game (not that I'm endorsing it, especially as he has gone into my handbag and emerged with my purse in his mouth; extracted a friends' scarf from his pocket without the friend noticing, taken half of my cheese and ham sandwich off my plate in a split second, helped himself to Jo's fish supper when she stood up to get the vinegar. I could go on, the list is endless); pushed the lid off a container containing loose biscuits and helped himself, Chilli and Mac pulled to the length of their leads to get there too and join in. Even blind dogs can be led astray. I only filmed for about a minute. Mac appeared to be looking at the biscuits, I presume he could smell them. He followed Harley, expert thief, and chief pilferer, determined to get his share of the spoils.

I don't feel too guilty about the shoplifters, we both spent quite a bit of money in there and they only managed to get a few biscuits each before we stopped them.

After his impromptu snack, Mac tried on his new coat for size. It was more like a woolly jumper, red cable knit, warm and pretty. I bought it. Taking it home my friend popped in. I showed her Mac's new coat.

Mac shook himself. It wasn't raining and it wasn't cold. He took himself off to his basket. He didn't want his new coat put on again.

My friend smiled and said, before she thought, 'he saw his coat!'

I raised an eyebrow and said nothing.

'Oh no, he couldn't have done.' My friend laughed. 'Perhaps he heard the word.'

Recalling how I had felt just after Mac's operation and what I had written.

Never to see the sun again.

No but he can feel its warmth and the soft summer breeze blowing through his fur.

Never to look into the garden and growl at the squirrels who dared to encroach on his territory.

He can hear them, and he still barks and growls.

Never to chase a ball again or find his favourite toy.

He didn't chase balls before he lost his sight but yesterday he chased a crow who came too near when the biscuits were being dished out. How did he know he was there? My son once said that crows have a dusty sort of scent, he thinks that if he can smell them, then he's sure Mac would be able to.

Also, Mac has started playing with his toys again. He finds them by scent and loves a good tug of war; he still growls and flings them about.

The best toys to buy are ones that make a noise, that crinkle or squeak.

Never to charge up the stairs, jump on the bed and sleep upstairs while he waited for the sound of the car, which meant his owner was home.

No, he won't do that, but he can climb up the stairs, he hasn't mastered going down them which is fair enough. I don't mind carrying him. He waits in his basket in the lounge if I've gone out and gets up when he hears me come in. Unerringly finding his way straight to me, standing up on his back legs for a fuss.

Never to watch the bees on the lavender and imagine eating them. (Mac was obsessed with bees).

All the better for the bees. They are a protected species! We can enjoy a walk in the summer without worrying about Mac snapping or trying to catch a bumble bee. He still enjoys his life and all his various walks.

Never to bark at or attempt to chase the neighbourhood cat, Dave.

I didn't want him chasing cats in the first place, unless they are doing their business in my front garden. Mac still barks at Dave or any other cat in the vicinity. He might not see them, but he can definitely smell them and erupts into a volley of loud barks. The first week after Mac's operation I remember thinking that if his blindness had a plus side, at least he wouldn't see a cat if it strolled into our street, then he wouldn't bark on our early morning walk and wake the neighbours. Fast forward six months, we walked out at seven in the morning, a cat was at the end of our street. For a split second I thought, huh at least Mac won't bark. Then he caught the scent and went mad, while I frantically tried to shush him.

Never to spot an item of food on the ground and pounce on it before I could stop him.

He'll find it. Especially if it's something he really likes. He is using his nose a lot more now.

Never to 'see' his friends again.

He knows they are there. He can kiss them and sniff them.

Never to see my face, or jump on mum's lap, or jump on the bed.

I'm sure he remembers what we look like. He sees us in his own way, He might not be jumping on mums lap, but he can be lifted up for a cuddle. When he's asleep sometimes his paws twitch and he makes those dream barks. Perhaps he can see in his dreams. I like to think so.

Never to chase the squirrels at Oldway.

No he won't. Unless one runs right under his nose, then he stands under a tree and barks. It's called 'barking up the wrong tree'.

I still have my little boy. It could have been worse.

For anyone else going through the same thing, it will get better. It is not nearly as hard as I thought it would be. You will cope.

One day you'll say, 'Oh I had a blind dog. It's no big deal. You'll be fine'.

Game, Set and Match. Winner: Macadoodle.

I don't know why I am using a few tennis terms as chapter headings except to say that in the early eighties my nickname was Mac, after my favourite tennis player, the American John McEnroe. Mac the dog was given his name in honour of him.

Playing matches, McEnroe would fight to the last point, as if it was a matter of life or death. Mac has that same fighting spirit.

It's five months since Mac had his remaining eye removed. It's winter and the early morning street walk is now undertaken before the sun rises; It's very dark and I can't see much more than Mac. I gazed up and saw all the stars and realised that I hadn't looked at the sky in weeks, having to keep my eyes on the ground, and on Mac to make sure that he wasn't going to walk into anything. The morning walk was relaxed and enjoyable again, for both of us. It takes a little bit longer. If Mac finds an exciting smell, he takes longer to sniff it, track it, and process the information. I give him the time to enjoy the walk in his own way.

Recently we went for a walk in Cockington. Mac was trotting off in front, following his nose. Every now and again I'd say, 'this side' and he moved across the path, away from whatever obstacle I wanted him to avoid. Or I said, 'careful' if he was heading towards a tree. He still went towards the tree but slower, I'd warned him it was there, but as I said before, he wanted to sniff around it.

Around a corner Sindy spotted a dog walker Mac loved, probably due to the fact that she carried dog treats. The lady was quite a distance away, but Mac started whining and ran off in her direction. Sindy and I were amazed. How did he know she was there? Did he hear Sindy say, 'there's your friend'. Or did he smell her?

I put him on the lead to go down the two uneven steps by the church. He acted as if he remembered there were two steps and was down them almost before I could give him a command. The next time we went, I didn't put Mac on the lead to do the steps. We stood close to him, one hand ready to guide him if it was needed, gave him verbal commands and he negotiated them with no problem, he'd obviously remembered our route.

Driving back from any walk in the past, Mac would shake himself when we were almost home readying himself to get out of the car. He is doing that again now. When we are about one street away he stands up on the back seat and shakes himself. How does he know where he is? All the places we drive to are in different directions and the length of time it takes to get to them, varies with each one. I take different routes depending on the traffic, yet he always knows when we are nearly home.

There is no doubt he is amazing. Sometimes we even forget that he can't see. My friends and I were talking about those first couple of weeks and how we'd had to watch him constantly, singing and clapping our hands so that he knew where we were. Now we just walk normally, chatting as we always used to yet keeping our eye on him as we do all the dogs. Mac stops now and again, and I tell him where I am, then he carries on, content in the knowledge that I'm nearby.

It's February, six months since Mac had his remaining eye removed. He is doing so well. He seems happy and content with his life. Having a blind dog is really no bother at all.

RECAP: Main tips to help a blind dog adjust.

Talk to your dog all the time, tell them what are you doing and what you are going to do.

Remember, your dog used to watch you constantly now he is listening, so talk to him.

It's important not to mollycoddle them. It's very tempting to do as much as you can to make life as easy as possible. Picking them up or putting them on the lead in the house might be quicker but it won't help them in the long run. They need time to get used to everything.

Wear a bell or use a clicker, then your dog can always find you.

Move things around your home as little as possible so that your dog can make a mental map of where things are. He may have lived in the same home for years but when he loses his sight he needs to adjust and find his way around using his other senses. If he is struggling, try using dog friendly scent markers.

In the first week, treat your house as if you had a toddler to protect. Cover sharp corners of tables and chairs with foam or bubble wrap. Use stairgates or block stairs so that your dog won't fall down them.

If he won't eat from his bowl try putting his food on a flat plate or a shallow dish.

If your dog used to sit next to you on the sofa, help him to jump up and jump back down, he'll soon get the hang of doing it without sight. With small dogs you can lift them up. I ask Mac if he wants to come up. If he does, he holds up a paw, indicating that he expects me to pick him up and place him on the sofa next to me.

On a lead walk, use the lead to give your dog signals, he will quickly learn to pay attention. Slight pull to the right or the left will indicate to him where he should go. Pulling the lead up to step up a kerb, saying the word 'up' as you do so. Tugging the lead in a downward movement to step off the kerb, saying the word 'down'.

In a similar fashion, when negotiating steps, keep repeating the words, holding the lead short so that you are keeping a tight control. With each step take it slowly repeating the word up or down until you reach the end. Then praise your dog and tell him 'all done'.

Your dog will quickly learn to listen to you and pay attention to hand signals via the lead. On an off lead walk use key words such as 'careful', 'this way', 'this side', 'over here'. Use the recall that your dog is used to, clapping your hands, or using a whistle, clicker, or bell to tell him where you are.

I've said it already, but it bears repeating, your dog doesn't know what is going on around him. Talk to him all the time, however silly it might feel. Tell him what you are doing, what you are going to do. Who is at the door. Who has entered the house. Listening to you and using his nose, will give him so much confidence.

His world now revolves around scent and sound, on walks, if you can, give him the time to enjoy the sniffs he is picking up.

About the Charities.

Mac came from Paws2Rescue.

Paws2Rescue have provided food, shelter, and medical care for thousands of stray animals in Romania and other countries and helped many find loving homes here in the U.K. At their heart, their neutering programme will cut down on the many stray dogs and cats trying to survive on the streets and avoid them being taken to shelters to be euthanized.

The charity have neutered over 16,000 dogs and cats in sixteen locations. They run educational programmes, have a winter campaign to provide food and shelter for as many animals as they can. The Christmas gift scheme provides clothes and treats for the children and elderly living in poverty in some of the more rural areas. Paws2Rescue provide veterinary scholarships to enable young people to train at college or universities in Romania. They do a great job and so many pets have now found loving, safe homes to live out their remaining years. Please check out Paws2Rescue website if you are interested in their work, would like to donate, or to find out more about re-homing an animal.

Battersea Dogs and Cats Home. London.

Jess came from Battersea.

At Battersea they aim to never turn away a dog or a cat in need of their help. They give each one lots of love and care, get to know their characters and quirks so that they can find them a new home that's just right for them.

All the knowledge they gather in their centres helps them improve the lives of animals they will never meet through their work with other organisations and charities including Paws2Rescue. They also help people make informed choices when getting a pet, provide training and welfare advice. They campaign for changes in the law when they see that dogs and cats or their owners, deserve better. They say that they want to be there for every dog and cat, wherever they are, for as long as they need us.

Check out Battersea Dogs and Cats Home website if you wish to find out more about them, donate, or re-home an animal.

About the author

Debbie Jefferies lives in Torquay, Devon. She loves reading, writing, wild swimming, animals and going for dog walks. Retired, she cares for her mother and her blind dog, Mac in the home that they share.

She has one son living nearby, who visits regularly to help his mother and his nan, also assisting in the training and walking of their dog, helping Mac to adjust to losing his sight. Thanks Damian.

She has written three romantic comedies and sneaked the dogs into all of the books.

Email: Debbie Jefferies Kiera38@yahoo.co.uk

Also by Debbie Jefferies

Sins

Captive by Moonlight

Greyholt

Available from Amazon.

Printed in Great Britain
by Amazon

38406146R00066